POET'S SOUL

MICHAEL LOVETT

Email: michaellovettwrites@gmail.com
Website: www.michaellovettwrites.com

Editor: Cam Johns
Cover Design: Touch Creations Designs

Dedication

Love you, like I love myself ...

Acknowledgements

I would like to begin by giving Thanks to God. Only through God would this all be possible. Special thanks to my Parents, Kerry and Kathy Lovett. Thank you for believing, and never giving up on me. Your Love has always been unconditional. To the both of you I owe everything.
To Michael Lovett II, Aka, Lil Mike. Son, I love you more than you can ever understand. I pray that all of your dreams come true. I am so proud of the Man you have become.
To Steven Lovett, I Love you. I'm still my Brother's keeper.
To Giselle Bello, Mi Amor. Baby, I am so blessed to have such an amazing woman like you. Never have I experienced love, sacrifice and commitment to the magnitude of which you've shown me. Thank you for your love, support and loyalty; life with you is beautiful.
Thanks to all the people who have touched my life in some shape or form. You have been my motivation and constant inspiration. To my Family, all my uncles, aunts, cousins and the loved ones who are no longer here with us. Thank you all for loving me.
Big thanks to the friends that have been with me through thick and thin. T.J., Ronnie and Claire, Mya Matos, Sean Malbrough, Steve Washington, Squeak, Marija Elias, G. Ward, L. McCoy, and many more whose names I may not have mentioned. I'll never forget you.
To the Fallen Soldiers... R.I.P. "Bear".
To those who may have sparked emotion in me due to our connection or experiences,
we good... .
Special thanks to Ms. Domita White @ A2A Publishing, and SWCO Magazine for publishing my work and introducing me to the World on your Podcast, *"The Stones Will Cryout."* Thank you.
To Mr. Maurice Clifton, Poet, and Author of *"Too Black",* thank you brother for pushing me to accomplish a major goal. Thank you for seeing the potential in me. You have been nothing but an inspiration and a positive influence. Thank you.
To my brothers, the Men serving out their time in jails and prisons across the Nation, you are not forgotten. Your Freedom is on its way, and when it comes to you, cherish it and use it wisely.

I pray that we all find our own happiness, love, peace and freedom. Last, but not least, I would like to give a special thanks to Author Cam Johns for helping me throughout this entire process of bringing my book to life. You have been invaluable with your advice and support. Thank you.

I am humbled and grateful. Thank you.

Sincerely,

Michael Lovett.

Table of Contents

Introduction

I have come a mighty long way. The struggle has been real, but it has not destroyed me, nor has it defined me. In other words, I have not become the product of my shortcomings and faults. Going through the fire has refined me.

Time has groomed me for the life that I was meant to live.

Time has led me to the doors of possibility.

Time has opened the walls of my mind, the door to my heart and the window into my soul.

Through time I stand a Humbled Man.

POET

Sometimes, I stare at empty lines on the paper,

holding a pen in my right hand as my thoughts

come and go like vapors, evanescence.

Waiting patiently to be enlightened or inspired

by love lost, and lessons learnt.

Treading in churning waters of regretful mistakes,

tirelessly searching for a way to make things right,

So I Break …

Scattered to and fro like seeds sown to dry dirt,

praying for rain, so that life might spring.

Forth from pain and hurt,

I seek my soul, deeply, in pursuit of self-knowledge

Like a sapling reaching for the sun.

And when I write I grow,

with each word I unveil my feelings

and innermost secrets.

Michael Lovett

Things my mouth would never let you know

But I relinquish my mind and pieces of my heart.

A poignant composition in verse,

with no fear, cloaked in love, washed in tears,

a creative artist of intense sensitivity.

Looking at the world through a panoramic eye,

yearning to give more of my life so I die all the time

Poetic Justice, a reincarnation of truth,

and all the greatness I can muster inside of me.

Beautifully my words manifest all that I am,

and all I believe, becoming incantations of verbal charms,

The Euphony of my existence, so *STILL I RISE*

like Maya Angelou...

My body bound, physically caged, but my mind climbing

Amazing Grace, trying to see how high I can go.

So I escape, letting the ink flow on sated paper.

Through me, creating poetry...

The Gift from GOD that sets me FREE...

INSIDE MY HEAD

I often lay on my back, gazing at the paint on the ceiling.

Drifting in reminiscent thought, and then suddenly,

being snatched back into the disgusting ...

and daunting reality of my confined existence.

So much regret, combined with the haunting

voices in my mind.

Constantly reverberating my mistakes, my misfortunes,

and time fleeting,

watching the years languidly leaving.

Hollow from shattered dreams,

and broken hearts still bleeding.

Now awakened, thinking outside the box.

Thoughts adversely fluid, while living inside the box.

Unbelievable how I see things so clearly now.

Provoking thoughts conjured from the depths of my mental

capabilities.

Michael Lovett

Ideas born from the creative gifts of God,

birth the answers to the questions,

I never cared to solve.

And I find myself, by myself, Here I am!

A soul in the body of a man,

suffering from the deeds of my own hands.

Sentenced to anguish by my choices and vices.

Alone in the land of the lost, among the Living Dead,

tired and too numb to be scared,

trying to figure out life inside my head.

Eyes open all night, sleep always escaping.

Conversations with God, negotiating my soul,

Seeking, Searching, Praying...

MY PERSPECTIVE

I don't mean to be inappropriate,

but when I think of you, I see you as you are …

standing before me naked.

All beauty complete and natural perfection.

But its not just your flesh, it's your eyes,

windows to your Soul.

Looking inside of you, and all I see is LOVE.

You speak to me, but not with your mouth.

It's your mind with all your sensuality.

Got me strapped down like I'm bound,

silent communication on every frequency,

got my emotions and feelings in a bind.

Waiting to hear you say, you love me,

but I say it first every time.

Speaking of Loving you, I just say it because it's true.

Discarding hesitation, so I cross every line.

Michael Lovett

I find myself dreaming about my future,

making plans to have you there with me,

I see you in every equation of my thought process,

I need you to trust the process.

Believe what you feel,

and know when I say that four letter word, its real.

LOVE; it stands alone, overcomes all,

overshadows the insufficient, every heart beat consistent ...

steady, unconditional, undeniable.

The glue that holds life together, the bone in your back.

I breathe and inhale all of you, your heat warms me.

My arms hold you, my hands like brushes,

painting pictures on your skin like canvas,

with each stroke a work of art,

open legs spread apart,

giving you everything you could ever want.

Nobody else even matters at this point.

No questions left unanswered, no doubt.

Erasing All Fear...

I JUST WRITE

Until my pen runs dry,

I will write what I can't say.

Not because I don't own the words to speak,

but I don't own the space.

I can't cover the distance between us,

and I'm not able to utilize the technology,

that would allow me to express what's,

inside of me, electronically.

I write on the white note pads, with black ink,

unveiling thoughts that provoke

ideas, deep thinking.

Stirring emotions, both inspiring and provocative,

stinging like bumble bees buzzing through me.

I write to you verses of love.

Mission statements of trust, promises,

decrees of loyalty, and prayers to a God

Michael Lovett

I believe in, but barely even know.

When you read my words over and over again,

It's almost like you can hear me.

I hate you sometimes, because I love you.

Insecurities getting the best of me.

Some prose I write I really don't want you to know,

so I ball the papers up, and toss them on the floor.

In search of peace and harmony ...

therapeutic, like psychiatric sessions,

read carefully, these are my confessions.

True realities of real life fallacies,

smiling to disguise the falsehood that every ...

everything is all good, but it ain't.

I paint pictures with the alphabet,

constructing run on sentences of what is

both beautiful and ugly at the same time.

The creator of goodness in my heart,

and the architect of darkness in my mind.

The tainted Shakespeare, diamond in the rough,

fresh out the mine, still I shine inside.

I may never appear clear, and that is clear,

but a diamond is a diamond all the same.

I am who I am, and if you have ever known LOVE,

then you know my name.

Intellectual with incorrect grammar,

vocabulary sharp like shanks and daggers.

Words that cut through the soul;

and then heal you with the power of the mind.

Miracles within each and every line.

Adjectives, nouns, verbs, all come together

to make you whole.

Until my pen runs dry, I will write what I can't say.

Just so you know...

Michael Lovett

MAN & WOMAN

I am just a man, in a place among men and monsters,

goons and crazies, lost souls, clowns and weirdos.

I am just a man whose light is dim,

but my fire within refuses to die.

I live and survive trying to let my little light shine.

This man that I am, yet flawed and scarred,

holds inside his chest, a golden heart pumping fearless blood

into rivers of love, flowing into my sea of troubled waters.

Nothing can stop the mighty power of love rushing

rapidly over rocks, cutting through hearts of rigid stone.

Just to reach the bottom of your soles where you stand,

to bathe your feet, to rise up over your calves,

and climb up your legs, and cover your waist,

to sweep you away, far away … right into my arms

smack dab in the middle of my life.

You are just a woman who long ago loved a young man,

got involved way too fast, made commitments that didn't last.

You made obligations to you and to me,

because you never tried to disappoint us, we have always been one.

Much too loyal to disappoint anyone else, save me and yourself.

You march on into the unknown, deeper, letting go

until you are swept away in the flow, moved by the rush,

drifting away in the mighty current,

tossed about in the waters of love.

Just a man, just a woman in two different worlds,

Hope and Faith combined, wanting the same things.

Sharing different pasts, trying to make smarter decisions,

wiser choices, for better futures.

Just a complex man, trying to love a simple woman,

with open minds and guarded hearts.

Mates of the same soul, lovers then and lovers now.

Rushing over the edge like waterfalls

above and below me, caught up in the flow.

Far away, but still so close, you have always stayed close,

lost and found in my love, let my love wash your soul.

Michael Lovett

Let God keep us whole ...

TROUBLE and PAIN

With roses comes thorns, and with pleasure came pain,

we were both young and wild, never meant to be tamed.

I wanted you close to me forever,

I tattooed your name on my chest, right on top of my heart,

relentless was our love, we couldn't' be torn apart.

So many time's you lay asleep while I held you,

and kissed your face, a beautiful work of art.

Watching you dream, wondering what you were thinking …

beauty sleeping.

I wish I would have been

everything I should have been, but I wasn't.

You told me, *only when I was not awake*

was I to be trusted.

But I kept on screwing up, and you kept on loving,

I was tripping, you were hurting,

I was cheating, you were weeping, crying

Michael Lovett

I was stupid, I kept on lying.

We were fussing and fighting,

then make up... and make love,

then lay in bed in complete silence.

I can hear your thoughts, its way too quiet,

it's cold we both know the fire is dying.

Without saying a word,

your body is telling me that you are sick and tired ...

you love me, but our time together is about to expire.

Letting go is a battle, a war between what is

and what was.

The space in the middle of

Love and Trust.

Knowing you need to let go, but you just can't.

You can't carry on living in the shadow of trouble,

loathing in the darkness of ignorance and desire,

thirsting for a taste of poison,

feening for everything you didn't need in your life.

Mister wrong just won't do right.

Trouble man, leading you down a road of pain.

Going nowhere fast,

this relationship is beyond repair.

I gave you roses, but the thorns pricked your hands,

I gave you rousing pleasure every time you called my name,

but it all comes with the price of Trouble and Pain.

Michael Lovett

I DIED INSIDE

I'm wide awake, I can't sleep.

Thinking of secrets that make me smile

and things that don't make me proud.

Remembering the feel of Love and Pain,

more hurt than love

until they begin to feel the same.

It's like everything that kills me,

makes me feel alive.

And then when you disappeared ...

inside I died.

WHO DO YOU THINK YOU ARE

Who do you think you are?

Remember it was almighty God who made you,

placed you inside the belly of a young Black Queen.

Barely seventeen,

October 10, 1973

Biological father, he gone, absentee,

left us all alone, he never met me.

Bow-legged happy baby, smiling oblivious

to the unfair cards that life had dealt me.

But God...But God...He smiled on me.

Who do you think you are?

When you got Mama and Daddy,

five sisters and three brothers in a 3-bedroom house …

you plus a baby, that's an extra mouth.

Formula and diapers, that stuff cost,

Kathy had to get a job.

Michael Lovett

Welcome to Churches Chicken, can I take your order?

Pretty smile, squinting eyes, hair cut in a bob.

Junior in High School with a baby boy,

and a part time job.

Who do you think you are?

They say a child without a Father is a bastard

then God gave me one.

Sent him right to my Mama's workplace,

in a Metallic Gold Ford Mustang.

Afro, butterfly collar, platform shoes,

and bell bottom jeans.

Thought he was the cleanest thing

the Southside had ever seen.

His name was Kerry Lovett, and he said,

Hey pretty young thing, this here what I need ...

a two-piece white, a roll, a pepper and a strawberry soda.

Hopefully a chance to get to know you.

Flashing that million dollar smile, with a $45 dollar gold tooth...

Huump...Negro please!

You come up here every week, flirting with them ol' tight jeans on,

and that shiny car that you think so clean.

But see that don't impress me

you see, I got more important things.

Like big dreams, like graduating,

Raising my son, giving him everything.

If you really want to be with me

You got to be ready to be a Daddy.

"A Daddy?"

I'm just sayin, it's a package,

my son comes with me...

Who do you think you are?

"I will", and he did, and his word was true.

And shortly there after they said, *"I do"*...

"I do", and I will love and provide and protect,

cherish and hold, now and when we are grey and old.

Forever and ever until death do us part,

I give you and Michael my name, my heart.

My Wife, my Son...

And he raised me like I was his own flesh and blood.

Young golden one, as if Lovett blood

was pumping through my veins.

"Michael Lovett", with pride I wore that name

"Who do you think you are?"

Things were great as far as I can remember,

birthday parties in October,

turkeys and sweet potato pies for Thanksgiving ...

bicycles and Rockit Sockit robots for Christmas.

Life is good, school was fun, summers were better.

"Boy you black", from all that hot Texas sun.

Football and footraces,

Second place was the beginning of the losers.

I always tried to be number one, born a winner.

Michael, get your tail in the house boy, it's time to eat dinner.

"Who do you think you are?"

A white man named Butch used to witness to my Father at work

everyday.

"Praise the Lord Brother Kerry, when you're going to surrender to God?

Come to Church with me brother,

don't you want to be saved?

"Leave me alone Butch, I ain't going to no Holy Roller Church…

(And I ain't your brother.")

It took months for my Dad to break down and go.

Persistence had my Father on a Sunday evening sitting on a wooden

pew.

And when the spirit began to move, the tears began to flow.

He gave his life to Christ, and received the gift of the Holy Ghost.

And our lives changed, it was like my Dad was a new Man …

a brand new Man marching to the beat of a new band.

He went from jamming the Ohio Players record "Fire",

Boom, Boom, Boom, Bada, Boom Boom, Boom

with a Schlitz malt liquor bull in his hand,

to dancing in Church, to *'It feel like fire, shut up in my bones, umm,*

hmmmmm …'

with a Bible in his hand …

"Who do you think you are?"

Michael Lovett

Church, Church, Church, Sunday School, Sunday night service …

Wednesday night bible study …

Thursday night prayer meeting, Friday night youth service …

Saturday Choir practice, singing in the Choir.

Playing the drums, acting in the Christmas play,

Guy___lee, man_____ …

Mama, I ain't going to church today.

"Boy don't play with me… you better get your Bible,

and get your butt in that car."

I was there even when I didn't want to be,

it was ingrained in me.

Church is who we are, even when we don't want it to be …

"I just wanna do me".

Gravity of the world pulling at me,

Pulling me, Pulling me.

"Who do you think you are?"

High school was a blur, I'm in College now,

got me a swisher sweet and a ice cold 40 oz.,

It's a party now.

Got me a girl, she's older than me, she's teaching me …

taught me too much, now I got a baby,

nineteen with a whole lot of responsibility.

I need a way to make more green …

I'm a Father, I'm a Dad,

my son the most beautiful thing I have ever seen.

How am I gonna provide for all his needs?

So I enlisted …

Boots and fatigues … push-ups, *"Get down, get up!!!"*

"Uncle Sam gonna make you tough."

"Your left, your left, your left, right left…"

"Oh, O_____wooh ohh"… Boots on the ground …

"Private why you eyeballin' me?" "You in the Army now!"

"Who do you think you are?"

Lured by the fast life, the Army was too slow.

I messed it up, Multiple article 15's,

the Army let me go …

Maybe the worst mistake I ever made,

because I gave up, threw my career away,

Michael Lovett

and I picked a sack up.

For the love of money, the things we do,

go against everything we ever knew.

It's got a hold on me that I can't break free,

and once I got my feet in that door,

all I wanted was more, and more and more.

And as the weed smoke blew, money rolled.

Every time them birds flew,

it took me around the world and I _____ya, ya ...

and I got the paper, and I got high, I had the women,

I thought I was fly, I made me a name,

a few times I almost died.

how did I even get here?

And who are you? And where did you come from?

And I'm tired of living a lie ...

And I'm tired of ducking the police ...

Looking over my shoulder ... I'm tired of being on the run,

And what have I done?

Why have I been to prison more than once?

And how is this my life? Why I got to pack a gun?

He a six time felon, oh he street certified!

Just to disguise the guise of shame and pain

I stay high on weed, pills, sippin' Styrofoam cups of codeine ...

And if they catch me with all these drugs and guns,

They might give me 15...

Is this a bad dream? 188 months, that's 15 ...

Who am I? This can't be me ...

Can't even really remember where it all went wrong.

This is my Song, this is my Song ...

The blues, my soul moaning, my heart crying ...

My feet stuck in muddy waters,

a free bird with no wings, caged away from the sky,

Caged away from my life ...

Hid away from my family,

removed away from my own self destruction

Stripped down to nothing, back to square one ...

to break the chains, to heal the pain,

to renew my mind, to save my life.

Michael Lovett

Just as my father saw His light,

He too dredged me through this worldly fight.

A internal struggle I needed Him to defeat.

But God, But God, he smiled on me.

He has set me free, free from the bondage,

free from addiction, free from myself …

He opened my eyes to see that I am nothing by myself.

Remember almighty God made you,

Created you, in His own image.

You thought you were somebody!

Oh you think you the man!

You thought you could do it on your own!

You ain't got no "power" in your hand!!!

"Who do you think you are?"

LOST LOVE

I'm still trying to understand love and all the pain that comes with it.

Days and days of pain flooding my heart,

Losing everything, left with nothing … but memories,

and confused emotions.

Dealing with the notion of moving on, rebuilding alone,

standing in my sorrows knee deep.

With a dark cloud hovering above my head,

reliving our last moments, thinking of what I should have said.

Alive in my mind, living in my head,

hanging on to the thought of you, even though I know

what we had is dead.

Finished, done, over, through!!!

Everything but the tattoo of your name on my shoulder,

like a chip on my shoulder.

Anger and bitterness setting in, wishing I didn't know you.

But I did, and I do, and it's hard to deny the truth …

Michael Lovett

I love you, and I hate you, because I love you

all at the same time.

You are all I see, and yet I am blind, to every other thing …

like you are the only color I've ever seen …

like you are the only one, the only thing.

Now my heart breaks and bleeds.

Dripping like raindrops, into puddles of Lost Love …

making ripples of regrets, Drowning in your flood …

ARDNAXELA

Beautiful woman, was I wrong for loving you?

It's been so long, maybe I should just let you go.

I know somebody has replaced me, kissing away your tears,

but nothing can take the place of you being near.

I wonder what you feel when I cross your mind …

no matter how good, memories still fade over time.

And I know I don't need you, but I want you.

Is it crazy to be holding on to someone who were

never truly mine?

Michael Lovett

THAT'S CRAZY

Born into darkness, made from the light,

I had everything I wanted,

but it came with a price.

I paid with my life,

I paid with my thoughts, I paid the cost.

That's crazy....

Listening to the voices in my head,

telling me to go hard, get money, don't stop ...

get more, come on, go ahead.

I did, full speed ahead.

Diving face first into such a mess of a life,

off the deep end,

falling into one hell of a tailspin.

Until I crashed and wrecked so fast,

I woke up and found my ass in the pen.

With 188 months, now that's fifteen!!!

10 years and 8 months, plus 60 months stacked.

Can you believe that?

That's crazy….

Fifteen years, 8 months, now I'm looking

for God to save me.

Save me from the guns, save me from the drugs …

save me from the prosecutor, save me from the Judge.

Just save me. Because I feel like my lawyer

and the United States Government straight played me.

Now I'm waiting on a chicken tray every Thursday,

and hamburgers were yesterday, every Wednesday.

Friday will be something different, I wish.

But it's the same old shit, we're having fish.

That's crazy….

Got me impatiently waiting for some letters,

I'm double checking the mail list.

Still waiting, nothing today from the woman I miss.

I sit, and I wait, and I sleep, and I wake.

Looking at nights turn into mornings,

31

Michael Lovett

and mornings turn into days, days turn into weeks,

and weeks turn into months, months turn to years.

And years turn to slow.

Every time my thoughts run,

I go over, and over the night this nightmare begun.

That's crazy....

Born in the darkness, made in the light ...

only if I could go back and change that night.

Everything would be different, things might be all right.

You can have all the power, all the money,

take it all, leave me with nothing.

I just want my Life ...

I just need the simple things ...

I just want a wife ...

But I don't need no fancy ring.

I just want a job, work boots and Levi jeans.

I don't need much, a little old house

and an old pickup truck.

Can I at least have that?

God do you hear me, can I have my life back.

Is that crazy?

Michael Lovett

NIGHTMARES

Looking between the lines,

deep in the corners of my mind.

In the darkness where dreams

quickly become nightmares, twisted,

haunted by some kind of mental sickness.

I keep on doing, the same things.

Blindly chasing riches,

giving love to unworthy bitches.

Oblivious to the realness, running from the goodness

Subconsciously tricking, never receiving,

always giving.

The walking dead, not really living,

incarcerated zombie, despicable me.

Trying to detach myself from the past,

almost doomed by the ghosts that loom over me.

The shadow of a black cloud crying on me,

salty tears of regret.

Mourning for the sake of sorrow,

for I cannot exist in the beauty of freedom.

While breathing the stale air of nothingness.

The void, the lonely emptiness of heartache,

too many mistakes, and unlucky breaks.

Broken by cursed words, spoken from evil lips.

Spawned by malice and ill-intent.

Watching from a bad place with envious eyes,

blatantly with no disguise.

While I live and die at the same time,

face to face with my fate.

Looking between the lines,

deep in the corners of my mind.

In the darkness, where dreams become

Nightmares....

Michael Lovett

LOST AND AIN'T KNOW IT

They said the Revolution would not be televised,

but they lied.

Because everyday I see protests, bloodshed, people die ...

riots, police, tear gas, bombs falling from the sky ...

Internet, Fox News, CNN Live, uprising, revolt, picket lines.

But we don't care, and we don't mind,

like they brainwashed our manipulated minds.

Destroyed our will to fight, no power to the people ...

because we forgot the difference between wrong and right ...

we're in the dark, blind with no light, no vision, no sight,

No Justice, No Peace.

In the streets like NWA back in the day,

and we still screaming, *Fuck the Police*.

Hoping they don't kill me,

because the color of my skin. I'll get life, never see my family again ...

If I stand my ground and fire my piece, Trayvon Martin Rest in Peace.

But I can't rest, and I can't sleep, because I'm in way to deep.

Looking out the window with my M-16,

Feeling like Malcolm X, by any means.

My reality is a nightmare.

Dr. King, what ever happened to your Civil Rights Dream?

I'm on some smash everything, *gimme the loot, gimme the loot,*

cream; cash rules everything around me ...

we thirsty, we hungry, feed me, more Gucci, more Versace,

cameras always watching, TMZ live, damn paparazzi, Can't Stop Me!

All gold everything, foolish lifestyle, everything but a King.

Hope these goons don't rob me, gang violence, drug wars,

Hollywood, movie stars. Who is your god?

FEDS giving us time, like we are drug lords.

My President is Black and White,

Just like all of them cop cars, light flashing colors red and blue,

like Crips and Bloods do.

And all my tattoos look like scars of money, women, and cars ...

the life I lived, calendar years, and inked tears,

crying for people starving ...

and the government spending billions,

trying to find life on Mars.

Children dying on Earth, and their Fathers dying behind bars.

Who gone raise them, show them love instead of hatred,

This is *America*, home of the *racist*.

Living the illusion, what are we doing?

Thinking slow, diamonds in our mouth, we the butt of the joke ...

everyday hustling, and a nigga still broke.

Selling all them cocoa leaves and tons of weed,

and we didn't even grow it.

Living lavish, spending habits, thousand dollar shoes.

See it, got to have it,

shit talking, still pimp walking and can't even afford it.

Genocide killing ourselves, we fucking and aborting,

can't you tell we lost as hell ...

And ain't even know it!

WHY YOU LIE

Does the truth ever come out of your pretty mouth?

Or do you utter delicate pink lies,

with your charming southern drawl

looking me right in ensnared eyes.

Surprising how your effortless allure captures me every time

Who do you think you are?

Baby I know who you really are, not

lying, faking, pretending, that you are real.

I was your guiding light, before you were a shining star.

But inside your fire is dying,

and I keep shooting my love to you.

I swear on life, I keep on trying

In every kind of way in which I can create,

still loving you until my heart aches.

Does it even matter at all, these silly games you play?

You said you would be there for me,

Michael Lovett

but where have you been ... where are you ... what did you say?

What do all your broken promises mean?

Idle words proclaiming things I can no longer believe,

every time you fix your pretty mouth to open and lie to me.

THE TRUTH

The truth is when you get slapped in the face with reality,

that stupid look you have fixed on your dumb face.

When you know you just messed up,

the uncomfortable feeling of being wrong.

When you swore on your life, and all that you love that you were

right...

but you were still wrong, dead wrong.

Truth is when you are all alone and you cry,

because you know who you really are inside.

It is when emotions overcome you, and you just let them.

You have reached your breaking point.

Truth is death,

knowing that life as it is, will one day come to an end.

When someone close to you dies,

then you realize you will never see them again.

The day the body is put into the dirt ...

void of a soul, becoming one with the earth.

Truth is how the world is always changing,

and how we as humans are always evolving.

Changing how we think and what we believe.

So far from spirituality, conditioned to live life based on

money, fame and technology.

Truth is unadulterated fact, strength and stability.

Something that is yesterday, today and tomorrow.

A forever thing, permanence.

Truth is the opposite of a lie,

And a lie can only exist, until truth exposes it.

The truth will set you free.

The Freedom to live your truth is Liberty.

Truth is what you know about what you feel,

when you hurt, when you lose what you once had ...

the karma, the payback. You reap what you sow.

Truth is when you look into the windows of the soul,

foresight, looking through flesh and beauty.

The truth can be found in the eyes where the story is told.

Hid behind a mask, reflections of pain, worry and heartache.

You can't hide what the truth has to say.

Truth is love unconditional.

Knowing that you are undeserving of Grace.

It is the Blessing of Life and the air we breathe.

Truth is redemption, it has no agenda, it is hard to hear,

it is hard to accept, it is powerful,

It is never sugarcoated, it is Undisputed.

It's Undeniable. THE TRUTH....

Michael Lovett

LOVE YOU FROM AFAR

I can love you from afar,

like looking into the Heavens at a twinkling star.

So many miles away, so many calendar days.

Complete separation, at a distance.

With no hesitation.

I can love you good,

you ask me how I could.

But the magic of love is not meant to be understood.

Standing like I've always stood,

With my arms wrapped around you, holding you so close.

Although I'm not there, my love is everywhere.

Even in the poems I write, and in the words you read.

My love can be found while you sleep,

living in your dreams.

My love touches your inner being, your memories.

Love is what you feel when you remember me.

When you hear my voice and your heart beats at a faster pace …

that look on your face, somewhere between here and that place.

That is where love comes from.

So on, and on, and on …

I can love you from sunset to dawn.

A love so strong, all night long, and early in the morning,

loving you like crazy, until you're tired and yawning.

This love is what keeps you going.

I keep it coming, never ending, forever flowing.

Like a mighty river rushing, love flooding,

touching every part of you.

Washing you away.

And the same power of love,

will bring you back to the very first day I loved you.

Surreal emotions every time, that tingle down your spine.

The thoughts in your mind …

the love that binds …

the space between you and I.

No matter where I am, or wherever you are,

Michael Lovett

I can love you from afar ...

OCEAN'S BOTTOM

Your love is like an ocean swallowing me whole,

pulling me into its depths,

sinking into never ending darkness.

Losing control of myself and all of my breath.

Until my lungs are filled with all of you

and all I see is blue, fading to black.

With the weight of love on my back.

I descend, falling into a liquid abyss,

closing my eyes as I remember the wetness of your kiss.

And as I go further, deeper, releasing myself,

the irony of drowning to death.

Your love is killing me softly, slowly, suffocating,

leading me to a watery grave.

Bound by thoughts of you, reaching for the light,

headed for the bottom, with no will to fight.

Unfathomable is your love, soundless ...

Michael Lovett

an epitaph of erogenous wet dreams.

Dying with you surrounding me.

And I go willingly, obliged by the numbness,

aroused by the danger of your obliviousness.

With good grace, earnestly I do choose Love.

For your puissance has taken me,

to the ocean's floor.

WHEREVER YOU ARE

I want to be wherever you are,

near you, close to you, in your mind, in your life.

My love is available, ready for you to indulge,

to receive, to experience, to engulf.

I need you to focus, to see me, to need me,

king me, queen of my heart, love and loyalty.

Standing by your side, steady, holding your hand,

side by side, never subtract, never divide.

You plus I, equals us, 360 degrees of trust …

a circle around you and me, love to infinity.

Something like forever, I pray we last that long.

With you is where I belong, in you I see no wrong.

Nothing compares to the feelings you stir inside of me.

I close my eyes and visualize your body on my body,

my lips on your lips, ears, neck, arms, legs,

all of you and everything in between.

Michael Lovett

I want to lose myself in you, so I can find myself in you.

Somewhere in your world, like a star in your galaxy,

floating weightless, coasting, soaking up your energy.

Giving you all my love constantly, never ending.

And for you, I will walk a million miles.

I'd climb the highest mountain, just to see you smile.

Just to be close to you, to give you what you need.

To be in your life, and to make you happy.

Let me be to you all that you've been looking for.

The One, your Friend, your Lover, your Protector …

your Rock, your Sun, your Moon and your Stars.

I want to be wherever you are …

BEAUTIFUL STORY

Dreaming of rainy days and nights, calm, fresh.

Watching as the drops fall and splash against the window.

Only in Mexico where the mountains look to the sun,

and the moon and stars shine and reflect on the waters.

Where Mother Spain left her kisses on the face of the land,

with Monuments of Faith, and Churches made of perfect stone

still stand in all their glory.

A beautiful place for a beautiful story.

Two people like night and day, two different places on God's Earth.

Brought together by no mistake, took my mind to Veracruz.

She painted me pictures of her world, so I could see her life.

Talking to me in a language I can't even speak,

but my soul understands.

My heart feels what you feel even from here.

In my busy city so many miles away.

Where the sun shines so hot on my dark brown skin,

Michael Lovett

the rain falls and still doesn't cool the humid heat.

In Houston, Texas where the buildings reach to the sky,

and the land goes as far as the eye can see.

But I see only you, trying to imagine how you must feel ...

wishing away the distance, looking at your pictures.

You could be my queen, lovely one, everything in my dreams.

Lying in bed, conversations until the early morning,

holding on to each word, not wanting to let go of the moment.

Falling in love like there is no wall between us,

dreaming of rainy days and nights calm and fresh.

DREAMS COME TRUE

I believe dreams come true ...

my flesh, my blood, I live through you.

I see more in you, a reflection of a better me,

being everything that I couldn't be.

My seed, the image of me,

my name, my smile, you are me.

My life, my heartbeat ...

I am the root, you are the tree.

Reaching for the sun, my firstborn son,

the apple of my eye, my pride, the golden one.

I pray that all you face, you prevail,

exceed and excel, where I have failed.

In life do right, and be strong,

where I have lacked and done wrong.

Be blessed with knowledge and long life,

love and be loved, this is wealth.

Michael Lovett

As life goes on, be true to yourself.

Spread your wings, see all your dreams,

beautifully come true, for me, through you ...

LOVE FACES

Looking at you is like dreaming with my eyes wide open …

spell-binding, simply beautiful, and I'm so happy that I know you.

I remember our first words spoken,

love at first sight, exactly right after the silence was broken.

The day that time stood still.

I feel like I'm still standing there, in that very place,

living in that moment, face to face.

Staring into your eyes, mesmerized, hypnotized,

emotionally baptized in your sea of seduction.

You were easy to love even before I ever touched you.

Clearly I can see that you were made for me …

handcrafted naturally by the Creator, especially for me.

Loving you with every part of me …

trinity, mind, soul and body.

And when we are together, every hour, every minute,

every second is miraculous, a love resurrection.

Michael Lovett

Living to give you all my love and affection ...

kissing your skin with lips of another complexion ...

color contrast, and blind passion ...

melting into pools of miscegenation, cohabitation.

Love making between persons of different races,

all we see is desire and anticipation on each other's faces.

Physiognomy, a reflection of what's inside of you and me.

And all I want to do is let my love adorn you ...

place all of my adoration upon you.

I don't want to stop living this way,

like I'm dreaming with my eyes open, wide open, so awake.

A beautiful reality is the love we make.

With each breath we take, our thoughts escape.

Leaving expressions of love written all over our faces.

Love faces.

1000 MORNINGS

For 1000 mornings I woke up with you on my mind.

The sun tip-toeing across the brand-new baby blue sky.

Barely awake, stretching, yawning, wiping the sleep from my eyes,

I look for you, I reach for you, but you are never by my side.

I want to lie back down, close my eyes and sleep,

so that I may wake up again still loving you for 1000 mornings.

The day is upon me, I cannot stay and sleep,

I think wide awake.

The memories I make are special to me,

the most beautiful thing I have ever seen.

Even before my life, here and after,

I will never love another.

Until the end of the world as we know it,

tomorrow plus 1000 more mornings, loving you.

You bring heat like summer, deep down in my stomach.

You make my heartbeat like crazy, speeding,

Michael Lovett

racing thoughts of you, contemplating us.

Irrational decisions and the question

of will you be there, with me.

When I look by my side, when the sun touches the eastern sky.

If you are not there, you will still be on my mind, for 1000 mornings.

RECIPROCATE

As you desperately walk the tight rope of love,

trying not to fall for me,

I wait down below patiently.

With my arms outstretched, reaching for you.

Forever to love, to hold, to protect, never to neglect.

I am what you thought you were looking for on the other side,

The faithful moon in your black sky.

Always just enough light to get you by,

No doubt, no fear, count on me,

I will be there to take away the pain.

With kisses for your tears,

I'm that guy who can love you easily.

Stop being blind and open your eyes so you can see.

Love has been here all the time,

always and forever, like you, on my mind.

I have never been hard to find.

Michael Lovett

I have never been short on love.

Still standing in line with my heart in my hand,

waiting for you to finally realize

I was sent here to be your man.

We were made to love,

you were made for me to love.

How else can I express the way I feel?

For you I would die, shed blood and kill.

You are my heaven right in the middle of hell,

how long will you ignore what is unmistakably real?

When we are together you can't deny what you feel,

I gave you my all, and that's a big deal.

And at the same time, that's a big leap of faith,

love me back, give what you take.

All I'm asking you to do, is reciprocate.

THE WAY I FEEL

It seems as though I'm overwhelmed by my emotions.

Like I'm drowning in love.

Everything that excites me, the life in me.

Who are you, and how did you come to be?

Occupying so much space in my mind,

when I'm wide awake, and even when I close my eyes.

You are there, way over there, and I'm here!

Spinning, round, and round,

as I go falling, falling for you … falling into you.

These feelings came out of the blue.

Dealing with trust issues, skeptical of my heart.

Making lustful wishes, looking into your lascivious eyes.

With desires of kissing your every part.

Every day, every night, under covers,

distant lovers, so far away.

So many things I want to say,

so many ways I want to touch you.

Loving you like you are all mine,

leaving your stomach full of butterflies.

Even though someone else stands between me and your heart.

I really can't care, I don't even mind.

This is a meeting of the souls,

a connection of the minds.

I want you like I want to give back this time,

like I need to be free,

I'm blind, and I need to see.

You are mine and you belong to me.

And when we talk, I want it to last forever.

I wonder if our feelings are the same,

because you are the perfect picture,

and I'm just a simple frame.

My tattooed arms wrapped around you,

holding you close, your breast pressed against my chess,

skin to skin, feeling you intimately.

Knowing you physically,

making love to you mentally.

Until we're tired, until we're done,

until we sleep.

Michael Lovett

PAIN IN MY SMILE

Pain in my smile, but I hide it so well.

Look closely, my eyes have many stories to tell.

Almost a lifetime filled with laughter and good times,

but in the confines of solitude, sometimes I pause and cry.

Too little truth and so many lies,

so much love and even more loss

experienced in pursuit of pleasure and success.

In search of something different, special,

on a quest for life's best at any cost.

My hands dirty from plastic bags of sparkling treasure.

A distorted belief that easy is always better.

Like economic freedom is owed to me.

Until I found myself riding in the back of a cop car.

Looking out the window at the life I was leaving,

Out of sight, out of mind, calculating the time.

Wondering do I ever cross anyone's mind, anytime.

So much time, for my crime, and I'm still doing mine.

Head to the sky, saying silent prayers,

wiping crimson tears from my eyes.

Angry as hell, with pain in my smile.

Michael Lovett

LOVE SPELL

Deceptive, young and beautiful ...

restless, wild and elusive ...

emotionally abusive, object of my desire.

Debative, persuasive, compulsive liar ...

never finish what she started, cold hearted.

Like a moth drawn to a flame, consumed by the fire.

In and out of my life,

I always fall for your type.

Everything about you I like.

You steal my love, like a thief in the night.

I see past all your faults, all I see is right.

All you do is wrong.

Can't get you out of my mind, thinking about you all day long.

Addicted to you like dope,

tied to the thought of you like rope.

Remembering all the promises you broke.

Heart breaker.

Sometimes I just want to hate you,

until I see you, or hear you, or feel you.

Then I'm loving you again.

Seducer, got me caught up,

dangerously falling deeper, going further …

a crazy, insane kind of love.

There is just something about you,

I don't know what it is, but I know I don't trust you.

I need to recover, get myself together,

and say, *"Fuck You",* for real, that's how I feel.

But you are still undeniable, mesmerizing and irresistible.

You have power over fools, but I see straight through you,

and at the same time, I never want to lose you.

A gift and a curse, for you I hunger and thirst.

Enticing love spell, unexplainable voodoo root.

You put something on me, got me hooked on you.

Consumed by your enchantment, and whatever magic you do.

Michael Lovett

Maybe something that belonged to me,

you buried in the dirt, 3 feet deep, beside the old oak tree.

Maybe something you cooked and fed to me.

Looked me in the eye and misled me.

I can never believe what you tell me.

But I feel what you're saying.

Sensual incantations, powerful energy, young with incredible beauty.

Careless and restless, got me out there loving reckless,

Scary, sexy, impetuous, so pretty, so poisonous, so deadly.

You put a spell on me.

THE SUN AND THE MOON

You are the Sun, and I am the Moon,

all that I am is a reflection of you.

Your radiance and light so brilliant and bright,

makes my cold dead rock, glow in the dark night.

Your heat and your warmth gives love faithfully.

Our love is forever, because you shine on me continuously.

Even the stars envy me in the background of its infinity.

My Sunshine without you, there is no me.

Michael Lovett

REDEMPTION

My eyes closed, lost in thought,

thinking of redemption.

Time keeps on slipping, days passing, fleeting,

praying to God, forgive me, change me, keep me.

As the world turns beneath me,

my feet keep moving, steady climbing.

Arms outstretched, hands trying to touch the sky,

determination to receive salvation inside.

Holding my candle in the sun,

so that my light can shine even in the daytime.

And all these people watching to see,

if the winds of life will blow out my light.

But I was built to keep standing, even after I fall,

and I was taught to keep fighting, even after I lose.

I was born to keep living, even when I felt like I was dying.

Smiling when my heart is crying.

Forgiveness for the life behind me,

loving myself for who I have become.

Turning struggle into experience,

experience into wisdom, emotional intelligence.

Love of self, this is wealth. REDEMPTION!

Michael Lovett

UNDER THE MOON

Under the moon we stood gazing,

both beautiful and amazing.

Stars in the sky reflecting in your eyes,

contemplating love and creation.

Here in the moment consumed

with feelings of elation.

As the universe and all that I am unfolds,

unleashing my soul into the wind.

As it blows gentle breaths of life into the Love we make,

until night breaks, bringing a new day.

And we taste the morning.

Because we've been awake with no regard for time,

good conversation, consummation, peace of mind.

A piece of me, and a piece of my mind.

We break-fast, sunny side up,

two full cups, black, one sugar.

Good morning, feeling optimistic about us.

I can see into the future and you are there, holding my hand.

Walking with me next to the blue sea, footprints in the sand.

Prophesy, unspeakable love,

beyond the world we know and understand.

Caught up in a blissful delirium,

daydreaming lost in thought.

Still aware of the precondition of my feelings,

untainted emotions dealing with the significance of the heart.

I find myself where I started in the beginning,

and at the end, in the same moment.

Standing in the cool of night, wrapped in moonlight,

omnipresent loving you everywhere at the same time.

Defining my experience through the passion

from which we create pure LOVE.

There is only One of Us, we are Love,

and the words that speak truth to why we exist.

Hearts hung high in the sky, causing an eclipse,

Michael Lovett

I will never leave you, I made vows,

promises of tomorrows, and right now.

Spoken fresh from our lips,

together forever might briefly end too soon,

holding you tonight, under the moon.

LOVE OF MY LIFE

Sitting alone just me and my thoughts,

intertwined with memories of our love.

My head spinning, my soul reaching,

and my heart forever beating only for you.

I'm missing you like crazy,

trying to fill the space and distance between us ...

so many years, months, and days held together

by love with no limitations.

Contemplating the possibilities of our relationship,

powerful, spiritual, simply amazing.

And you are as beautiful as a glistening night sky

still you shine, the twinkle in my eyes.

I know that God created you with me in mind,

a love that transcends time.

Counting down the days until I can hold you

and be by your side,

with every ounce of appreciation and dedication.

I honor you, because you stayed faithfully by my side.

My wife, the other half of me, my friend, my everything ...

my future, my past, my first, my last.

My diamond, my pearl, the Queen of my heart,

forever my Girl.

Bound together until the end of time.

I live for you, Love of my Life.

EVERYTHING TO ME

You are everything to me,

the stars on the face of the night.

You are the wind that blows the rain

when the sky cries.

When everything is wrong, you are everything right,

my candlelight, the ambience of love.

You intoxicate me, my favorite drug.

I'm addicted to your touch and the way you feel.

Being wrapped in your warmth is like

the sun kissing my brown skin.

My soul reaching for your soul deep within.

You are everything to me,

the air I breathe, love soaring, gliding

on every breath.

You lay beneath me like the earth

in all her beauty.

Michael Lovett

The rhythm of the universe,

music to the song of life.

I can hear your body sing to me,

every lyric, every verse.

Love moving through me all the way

down to my bones.

You are everything to me ...

my dreams, my passions, my thoughts,

all that is inside of me, my future, the one,

the life that is to come.

Looking at love from every angle, my geometry ...

we mix together, a perfect chemistry.

Shining rays of sunlight

in the windows of my daydreams.

All that I feel, all that I see,

my rock, my joy, my peace, the key to my lock,

opening the door to the knowledge of love,

and all it is, and all that it means.

You are everything to me.

BECAUSE YOU LOYAL

You bring out the best in me.

You love me with all my flaws.

Every little idiosyncrasy,

each and every scar on my flesh.

Each mole, and every ugly tattoo.

You love me like you love yourself,

selflessly giving everything, all of you.

Your purposeful hands gently grasping me,

constant, faithfully, even when I don't deserve you.

When I messed up and betrayed you,

forgiveness always found me.

Never ending unconditional love,

your loyal heart beating for me constantly.

Michael Lovett

YEARNING

I'm yearning for your body, hot and burning …

pain freaking, heart beating, hands reaching

for your femininity and every part of your physicality.

Both eyes closed as if in a dream,

a non-entity, being my reality.

Defining your sexuality in a mosh of uninhibited rhapsody.

In all actuality there is nothing between us

but space and opportunity.

Let's do it blind folded by the dark, void of light.

Your body is a book written in braille,

my hands are my sight.

Flipping through your pages and you look amazing, tonight

all I see is you engulfed in love.

Covered in kisses, drowning in lust.

Me in the middle with every single thrust,

you lay wet beneath me, with each drop of sweat.

While I push and they drip and splash on your breast,

and I've become aroused to the sound of sex.

Like the smack of our skin when our bodies

crash and wreck.

And the moan you make when my lips touch your neck,

then I push and retract.

You pull me in as you arch your back.

Your eyes roll back while you claw at my back.

I turn you over and thrust from the back.

You look at me and throw it back,

And back, and back.

Until we reached this climax,

Until we change the climate.

We're both relaxed, and we're both smiling.

Then we drift away and fade to black, black, black...

but before we are gone too far, we reach for more, more, more...

chasing passion into infinity and beyond,

feeding fuel to the fire, and light to the sun.

My trigger finger itches, and you are my gun.

Michael Lovett

I scratch, I pull, and bullets do fly,

Caressing my body, impact, the bullseye.

You are on target every time, killing me,

leaving me yearning for your body,

hot and burning, pain freaking, heart beating,

hands reaching for your femininity.

And every part of your physicality.

BOUND TO YOU

Obligated to your existence, your essence,

all of you, I'm tied to.

Twisted, mentally uninhibited, merged, two of a kind, combined,

speaking the same three words at the same time.

I Love You …

You said it with your eyes, I told you with my mind.

Telepathy, psychologically intertwined, bound to me,

body-to-body, heat and heartbeats.

I know passion because I felt it,

fire and desire, synched together slowly melting.

Love dripping, fingernails digging in flesh,

hands gripping and slipping from the sweat.

Prisoners of each other, shackles on our wrist.

Locked down...

And I know you from another place, kindred spirits,

soulmates.

Michael Lovett

Like I remember your face,

Beautiful angel from somewhere far away.

Like I can't forget your face.

Love from another Life and Time.

Got me feeling like I'm way to high, out of my mind.

Caught up, hooked on your line.

Viciously snared, trapped, confined.

Strapped to love and whatever comes with it …

joy, pain, grief, I accept with no regrets.

Give me no relief, I refuse to be released.

Ropes and chains calling my name.

Keep me tied to you, twisted, combined, intertwined.

We do what we do, this is our lives …

the love that binds, forever mine.

Synched together, melting,

love dripping slowly to the ground.

All of me, all of you, bound …

I KNOW WHAT LOVE IS

I know what love is.

Love is the sound of your voice speaking my name.

I can hear it and it always sounds the same, sweet to me.

Before you there was feelings, and attraction, there was lust and sex.

Now there are butterflies in my stomach, and fire in my chest.

I know what love is.

Love is your forever faithfulness, constant, like time.

Yesterday, today, tomorrow, and after I die.

Wherever my soul goes, I'll be waiting for you

somewhere still loving you. From a distance.

I know what love is.

Love is your skin next to my skin

soft and warm, your lips soft and moist.

Under the covers, in between the sheets ...

holding you, legs linked, rubbing feet.

I know what love is.

Michael Lovett

Love is your selflessness, your patience, your loyalty.

How you give me everything without question,

holding back nothing.

You come to me when I call with no hesitation.

Love and adoration,

completely surrendering your heart, all of you.

I know what love is.

Love is you ...

ETHEREAL LOVE

Somewhere in the dark shining bright,

like a star in God's black night.

Chasing your soul through the universe,

eager for a drop of you.

Wanting to quench my thirst.

I follow until you relinquish all that you are,

and all that you know, an incarnation of love

in thought, in word, and deed.

Something divine wrapped in outer beauty.

And you are mine, preordained by a higher being.

My soulmate, my energy, the air I breathe ...

the truth in me, my love, my everything ...

below and above, my past and my future.

I loved you before I ever knew you,

even more now my feelings are incessant.

Every part of me lives for you,

down to the smallest molecule.

Beyond what eyes can see,

you will find traces of love. In my DNA

you will find love in my blood.

Here and now I adore you, standing in abeyance,

as the world moves around me in a transonic blur,

experiencing the physics of love

and all that you are, surreal and dynamic.

An ineffable expression of the tongue

I speak with my mind,

telling you about love, a love that transcends time,

I laugh and sometimes I cry.

Releasing emotional joy that flows from my soul.

Behold all of me I do give

with each heartbeat and every tear,

loving you supernaturally without a trace of fear.

As we are now, and beyond the dirt,

here after flesh, and all that hurts.

You and I, here and there,

all of the space between Heaven and Earth.

Sharing the truth of love,

and the oneness of us...

Michael Lovett

YOU

Thoughts of you keep elbowing their way

to the front of my mind,

ideas of a beautiful union.

You are in my life by no mistake,

to not be persistent would be my worst mistake.

I can't lose my moment,

I can't miss the opportunity to close the space

between the two of us.

If only you could believe in love and trust.

If you could just let your guard down,

see that I could help ease the pain.

My tender care can take away the hurt.

In time, my love will make it all disappear.

Let me love you and show you that truth

lies in the aftermath of chaos.

Embrace what you feel and live it.

See me like I see you; Insight.

Remember how we first met; Hindsight.

I'm still looking for you; Foresight.

Day and night, thinking of how to get home to you.

I'm trying to get closer, closer ...

I'm trying to show you that you have my full attention.

I want us to share untold secrets,

and protect each other's confessions.

I just want to take away the pressure,

help make life a little bit better.

Whatever it is you need from me, allow me to give.

I only want to be with you.

For your love is why I live ...

Michael Lovett

PERFECT STORM

Unexplainable, supernatural love,

emotional high every time I look into your eyes

I'm crazy over you, so amazed by you.

Giselle always on my mind,

tattooed on my skin, te amo, bilingual

speaking love in two languages.

And I can't stand to be apart from you,

I'm addicted to the magic of your touch,

consumed in a whirlwind of your perfect storm.

You blow me away, bending me to your will,

uprooting me from all my past,

moving me closer to true love.

An undeniable attraction, magnetism,

pulling me closer to you.

My heart beating, rumbling like thunder ...

an electric connection, reaching, surging.

Sending bolts of love through me,

Like lighting, striking brightening up my life …

Michael Lovett

LOVE IN THE CITY OF LIGHTS

She was from the city of lights,

what happens there stays there.

It was simply amazing, a beautiful situation.

We agreed to make it last forever,

so I placed my heart on the table.

Engaged in conversation,

making love verbally,

plans for her to be with me.

She told me about her dreams and trust issues,

intimate secrets buried away like treasures.

Said I was cut from a different cloth,

I unfolded myself and unraveled on her,

spoke of truth so real into her ear.

Made her shiver, made it tickle good,

like Q-tips do when they go in deep.

We talk, and we laugh until we go to sleep,

then we both meet up in our dreams.

In my mind we can do anything,

in my arms she feels like everything.

Scorpio, got me smitten, overwhelmed by the sting,

intoxicated by all of her flesh and soul,

make me want to run away in the dark of morning.

To escape to secret locations, and explore private places,

making true all the desires and expectations we created.

As it is, and how it was written,

as God is my witness.

I stole her heart like a thief in the night,

from the beginning I knew we would be together.

Heaven in my eyes, love in the city of lights ...

Michael Lovett

NEVER

Never ever have I ever

felt love on this level.

Blind love, walking by faith

and not by sight.

Follow your soul it never lies,

faithful even after I die.

I knew what to do, I always knew ...

maybe my heart always belonged to you.

Still amazed by the energy

that pulsates through me, with the thought of you.

I am where I always wanted to be,

wherever you are, loving you from afar.

Emotions attached to the intimate memories

of the last time I felt your touch.

And it's like I'm right there,

hanging on to a glimpse of you,

I can still recall the scent of you.

Something I 've never experienced in all my years,

Never ever have I ever

felt love on this level.

Never...

Michael Lovett

ONE STEP AWAY

One step away from the unexpected,

eyes fixed on the rearview mirror.

Haunted by reflections of the past,

last year, last time, the other day ...

being in the moment; standing in my own way.

Never turned out to be what I expected,

ignoring the caution signs.

Will I? Can I ever? Before I die.

Not to be so pessimistic,

still trying to make reality out of my

dreams and visions.

Living to be more than what I am,

dying to have more out of this life.

Who promised us justice and prosperity?

Tell me why I've been working my

fingers to the bone.

Scratching away calendar days

like losing lotto tickets.

I can feel it; like its within my reach,

at any moment; right around the corner

it could be my time, struggling, striving,

trying to survive.

Holding my head to the sky, steady moving

one foot in front of the other,

this could be it, or it can be over.

Balancing the weight of the world,

praying for a major breakthrough

trying to get over; now I feel closer.

One step away from the unexpected.

About Michael Lovett

Poetry has been a part of me from an early age. I remember my third grade teacher reading Shel Silverstein to our class, and being so intrigued by the flow and intricate rhymes of the work. However, it wasn't until the 8th grade when I began to write poetry. I've always considered myself a romantic, so I would write love letters to girls that turned into poems … I thought I was Romeo.

Once in high school, my Theater Arts teacher Mrs. Holmes introduced me to influences such as Shakespeare, Langston Hughes, Gil Scott Heron, Maya Angelou, Nikki Giovanni, James Baldwin and Toni Morrison. From then on I was hooked, so I adapted my own rhythm of poetry. I would write all the time, on anything, whenever I was inspired or fascinated by a muse. It seemed as if I continued to be either sad or in love. So I wrote of only those emotions until discovering pain and heartache. I was also inspired by movies like "Slam" starring one of my favorite poets Saul Williams, while the movie "Love Jones", compelled me to attend poetry clubs mocking Larenz Tate. Poetry made me feel cool and allowed me to say what I was feeling.

I continued writing off and on throughout the years, but after I was incarcerated in Federal Prison in 2011 I wrote more fluently, as it became my solace. It's like I had so much to say … so much emotion … so many feelings. After all, when you are cut off from family and significant others, you will desire an outlet. Being imprisoned has allowed me to grow, explore my existence, my experiences and create something that was derived from deep within.

Poetry has become a sanctuary for my mind … my Freedom.

www.ingramcontent.com/pod-product-compliance
Lightning Source LLC
Chambersburg PA
CBHW061752020426
42331CB00006B/1439